Supertrucks

Pat Kennet

Illustrated by

Denis Bishop

SCIMITAR 57-59 Long Acre, London WC2E 9JL

Evijäri 370

All about trucks

Almost everything around us, from our food to our furniture and our clothes, is carried by truck on its way to us. In Britain, for example, nine-tenths of all goods are hauled by trucks at some stage; in America the figure is even higher.

Trucks come in all shapes and sizes and can move everything from bulk tanks of petrol to refrigerated containers of food and flatbed trailers loaded with giant pieces of machinery.

One reason why they are so widely used is that they can take goods to exactly where they are needed with no handling or shunting on the way. Whereas goods carried by boat, train or plane have to be taken at least part of the way by truck – to docks, stations or airports.

The heavy truck (below) is a Sisu from Finland. Due to the extreme climate and the tough terrain in which it operates, the Sisu has to be very rugged.

Finland has only a small railway network. Most heavy material for building sites must be carried by road. This Sisu is powered by a big 260hp engine and has a 15-speed gearbox. The tyres have special treads for travelling on dirt and gravel roads. There are two axles at the rear of the truck to help bear the weight of the giant loads it carries.

Articulated truck

Trucks fall into two main types — rigid or articulated. Articulated trucks (left) have the driver's cab on a separate 'tractor unit'. The trailer, which pivots on the rear part of the tractor, carries the load. Rigid trucks (below) carry both the driver's cab and the load on the same chassis. Rigid trucks can also be hooked up to trailers that are towed behind.

Rigid truck and trailer

At the wheel

The cab of a big modern truck is built for the safety and comfort of the driver. The dials and gauges on the dashboard allow him to keep a constant check that all parts of his machine are running smoothly. Truck driving is a tough job that can involve long working hours and often dangerous road conditions. The driver must always stay alert to ensure that his truck with its valuable load arrives safely at its final destination.

The average cost of a new truck is about £30,000. Its load can easily be worth more than twice that amount. Drivers have a big responsibility, and are well paid for their skills and hard work.

Tachometer   Tachograph

The picture of the inside of a truck cab (left) shows a Fiat 170 that was made in Italy. The big dial on the dashboard is a tachograph. It measures how fast the truck is going. It also records how long the truck has been travelling and shows when the driver stopped to take breaks. The other big dial contains gauges that show engine temperature, air pressure of the braking system, engine oil pressure, and fuel level. Another dial, the tachometer, shows the engine speed in revolutions per minute (rpm). This is very useful when working with a 13-speed gearbox. Lights and signal switches are all within easy reach of the driver.

Sunshield

Extra lights

Air horns

Sleeper compartment

Exhaust stacks

Home on the road

Drivers who spend much of their lives on the road have as many home comforts as possible with them in their cabs. Some cabs even have a bed for the driver. These are called sleeper cabs. You can easily recognise a sleeper cab because it is longer than an ordinary one. The sleeping part is behind the driver's seat. Usually there are two beds or bunks, for often these long-distance trucks have two drivers. In the cabs there may also be a cooker, a refrigerator, a portable shower unit and a locker for clean clothes.

Every long-distance truck has a normal radio and some have a citizen's band (CB) radio too. This allows the driver to talk to other drivers on the road and warn them of dangerous weather conditions, traffic jams or accidents. There may even be a small TV set in the cab, but it must be out of the driver's view when he is driving.

This American Kenworth VIT tractor unit has a sleeper compartment behind the main cab. The steering is power assisted and the gearbox has 15 speeds that enable the truck to tackle all kinds of work. An air-conditioner keeps the cab at a comfortable temperature in all weather.

KINGLEY IMBER LTD.

KI LTD

KI LTD

HHG 147 N

CILLA

8

Container trucks

Until quite recently all goods shipped from one country to another had to be constantly loaded on and off ships and trucks, like the one shown here. Many of these trucks are still in use. But today a lot of freight travels in big steel boxes called containers. Containers are filled at the start of a trip, then sealed. They can travel like this in trucks, trains and ships across the world without the contents ever being touched.

The big British built Atkinson Borderer truck (left) is about five years old – quite young for a truck. The container is bolted to the chassis and wheels of the trailer to make a single unit. This means it cannot be lifted off the trailer. So if this kind of truck goes overseas, it goes by 'roll-on roll-off' ferry. Most modern trucks carry the containers on flatbed trailers. The container can be lifted on and off the truck and stacked in the hold of a container ship with the cargo still sealed up inside. This means the cargo arrives in perfect condition at the end of its journey.

The body of a bulk carrier is very big and light. The aluminium 'Samson' trailer (below) has an hydraulic ram that tips the trailer backwards to empty it.

Bulk carriers

Raw materials like ore, grain or stone take up a lot of space in a truck. So, when they have to be moved, trucks called bulk carriers with big bodies and high sides are used. Often when light material, like coke, is carried boards are added to the sides of the truck so more can be loaded at a time.

When a bulk carrier has a light load, planks are added to the sides. Truckers call these 'greedy boards' as they allow a bigger load to be carried.

Greedy boards

The Mack truck (left) is an articulated truck. It is ideal for hauling bulk coke because it is light, powerful and very easy to drive in tricky conditions. Macks are made in America, but their little bulldog mascots are famous all over the world.

MACK

R·J·NORMAN

ODK833 R

Tippers and dumpers

The Foden (left) is a heavy dumper. It can take a 25 tonne payload in its big dump body with ease. The engine is powerful enough to let it charge over soft sand and gravel and plough through clinging mud. It is ideal for working on big construction sites and in open-cast mines.

Tippers and dumpers move rock, earth and rubble. Tippers work mainly on the road carrying materials to and from building sites. Dumpers work more on locations like mines and quarries.

These trucks have the rear end of the body hinged to the chassis. Hydraulic rams under the floor or at the front of the body lift it up so the load slides out. The rams are powered by an oil pump driven by the engine. The pump is switched off while the truck drives along, so the load cannot tip out by accident. A tipper usually has a 'tailgate' to stop the load falling out. A dumper has a forward-slanting floor called a 'scow end' instead.

The six-wheeled Ford (left) is a big tipper. For the most part, tippers are lighter and less rugged than dumpers. The conditions in which they work are less tough and the loads they carry are smaller, although the Ford shown here is able to haul about 16 tonnes of gravel.

FORD

APC 133 T

Off-the-road trucks

Special trucks are needed for working in places where there are no roads. Men who have to go miles off the road into the wilderness to lay pipelines or erect power cables drive trucks fitted with fat tyres that can grip in wet and muddy conditions. The engine drives all the wheels so that the truck can scramble across very rough ground. The floor of such trucks is higher off the ground than normal. This is so that the bottom of the truck won't hit tree stumps and rocks when it travels over very rough country.

The Scania SBAT111 (right) has six-wheel drive. This means the engine drives all six wheels. The Bedford TM—4x4 (left) is used by the British army.

Military trucks

Armies use special trucks to transport heavy equipment. Transporters are used to carry tanks over long distances to save wearing down the tracks. They are also needed to rescue broken down tanks and can be driven far off the road to unload the tanks in secret.

This Oshkosh M911 is a tank transporter belonging to the US Army. It is a special military version of one of the toughest trucks made in America. It can pull loads of up to 122 tonnes on its multi-wheeled transporter. Tanks can be hauled on board by winch.

Military trucks have all kinds of special fittings for carrying weapons and ammunition. In wartime they have sometimes been armoured and fitted with light machine guns. These trucks must be able to run on different kinds of fuel because normal supplies may not be available in war.

Logging trucks

Countries like Sweden that have a huge timber industry need special trucks to carry enormous logs from the forests to the sawmills. Usually these are six-wheeled trucks towing eight-wheeled trailers. Together they can carry a load of over 35 tonnes of wood. It takes highly skilled men to drive such trucks.

Often the trucks are fitted with a hydraulic crane so the driver can load up from great stacks of logs left in the clearings by the lumberjacks.

The Swedish logging truck (right) is a Scania LS141. The total weight of the fully-loaded truck and its trailer is about 55 tonnes. It takes a 380hp engine to move it. The Scania is unusual as it has a bonnet over the engine. Most modern trucks have the cab over the engine making the front flat.

The Scania (above) has three axles, and the trailer four. All the wheels except the front pair have twin tyres making 26 tyres in all. Each of these tyres costs about £150.

Fire trucks

Airports and many big industrial plants, like oil refineries or chemical works, have special fire trucks. A modern airport crash tender weighs about 28 tonnes but can reach over 80kph in 30 seconds. It travels cross country almost as fast as on roads. On arrival the biggest foam 'cannons' can pump over 60,000 litres a minute onto a fire. The foam consists mainly of carbon-dioxide bubbles which smother flames. It is made by mixing together two chemicals as they are pumped through the foam guns. Foam or powder are used to put out industrial fires instead of water because water is useless on burning petrol or chemicals.

Escape ladders are used to rescue people from tall buildings. These are controlled hydraulically. They can reach as high as 45 metres yet, when collapsed, they fit snugly onto the back of a truck.

The Benson (below) is commonly used to reach fires in tall buildings and rescue trapped people. The Carmichael (left) works as an airport fire and crash tender.

The Kenworth heavy
tractor (above) is
pulling a low-loader
bogie with 64 wheels.
It is carrying a giant
turbine for a power
station. The low-loader
has a specially powerful
hydraulic suspension to
help it over uneven
surfaces. The tractor has
all-wheel drive for extra
grip.

'Abnormal' loads

Giant pieces of machinery that are too big for railways have to be moved by road. Loads of 500 tonnes or more can be carried on trailers called 'bogies' fitted with up to 120 wheels. One powerful tractor pulls in front while another may push at the back and help to steer; manoeuvring is tricky.

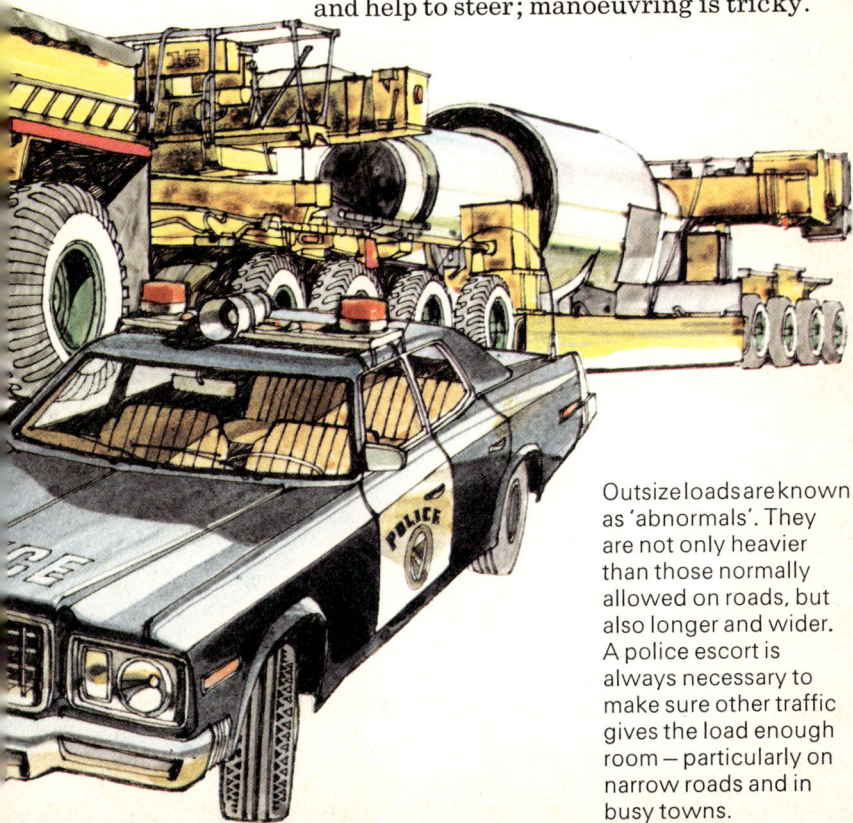

Outsize loads are known as 'abnormals'. They are not only heavier than those normally allowed on roads, but also longer and wider. A police escort is always necessary to make sure other traffic gives the load enough room — particularly on narrow roads and in busy towns.

Desert trains

When oil was discovered in the Sahara Desert, problems arose because ordinary trucks could not drive across the soft sand. So, special oilfield trucks were designed to do the job. These have unusually powerful engines, and tyres that work rather like a camel's foot and ride on top of the loose sand. The tractors have all-wheel drive to prevent the truck from getting bogged down in soft spots. Special seals and filters keep sand and dust out of the engine and a very big radiator helps keep it cool. The cab is air-conditioned for the comfort of the driver.

Trucks like this can pull loads of over 40 tonnes of oilfield equipment across the desert. Often there are no roads or even tracks to follow. Every truck is fitted with a two-way radio so that the crew can call for help if they land up in trouble.

A superb truck for desert work was specially built by Volvo for the oilfields of Algeria. The engine is a 350hp turbo-charged diesel with huge air filters. The tractor has all-wheel drive and a 16-speed gearbox to get it through the worst terrain. Heavy drilling equipment for the oilfields is loaded in the long trailer behind.

When there is no loading crane available, really heavy machinery can be winched on board the trailer by sliding it over the tail-end roller.

The long haul

All over Europe you can see trucks carrying a blue plate with the letters 'TIR' on it. They stand for Transports Internationaux Routiers. This shows Customs Officials that the vehicle has been approved for international transport and does not have to be checked at every frontier.

Under the TIR system a truck is checked by Customs at the start and end of a trip. It can then cross all frontiers on its way just by showing its papers and seals.

In most European countries TIR trucks have a maximum weight limit of 38 tonnes. Recently TIR haulage has been extended to the Middle East. Though the route is a good 6000 km, and often over poor dusty roads (below), it is quicker and cheaper to run freight overland than send it by ship. Today this route is one of the busiest in the world.

One of the most popular trucks used for long-distance runs is the German MAN (left). It is very economical and has a quieter engine than most big trucks. It is able to haul enormous loads of up to 100 tonnes.

The Yukon trail

In the very northern parts of Canada and Alaska, trucks often have to work in sub-zero temperatures. One big problem is that diesel fuel freezes at very low temperatures, so the fuel tanks have to be heated. Covers, like the one on the Kenworth (right), are put over the radiators. Also, batteries do not work well in extreme cold, so trucks have to be provided with much bigger and stronger ones than usual. Many truckers leave their engines running all the time as it is very hard to start them when the temperature plunges to −40°C. The driver's cab has its own oil heater.

The Kenworth (below) is hitched to a tanker trailer. Behind it, a mineral dumper is being towed. This is typical of the huge loads pulled in the Yukon.

The outback run

Trucks are the main lifeline for remote towns and villages in the Australian outback. Here, giant 'road trains' are used to haul supplies.

Road trains are made up of a rigid truck pulling a maximum of three 'dog' trailers, or an articulated truck towing no more than two trailers. The overall length of a road train can be as much as 45 metres; this is the maximum length allowed. Their weight when fully-laden may reach a staggering 138 tonnes.

Australian trucks often have tough steel frames bolted to the front bumper to protect them in collisions with animals. As the most common large wild animal in Australia is the kangaroo, these frames have become known as 'roo bars'. A kangaroo can damage a truck badly in a crash.

Most road trains are restricted to travelling on unpaved roads where the traffic is much lighter, so they are fitted with special dirt-track tyres. They throw up great clouds of dust in their path which can be seen for literally miles.

Three-unit oil tanker road trains (below) can carry over 100,000 litres at a time. Engines of at least 350-400hp are needed to pull such enormous loads at speeds of up to 80kph. A complete train can cost as much as £95,000 to buy.

The personal touch

Many trucks are owned by the men who drive them. Often they like to give their machines a personal touch that makes them stand out. This is called customising. The cab may be painted in bold colours and striking designs, and special gadgets like extra lights, windscreen visors, mascots and headlight shades added. Parts like bumpers, airhorns, exhaust stacks, air filters, fuel tanks and wheels may be in chrome or polished aluminium.

The owner-driver of this American Brockway has customised it with a distinctive paintwork of stars.